DOG HOME

written by Sue Grayson
illustrated by Laurie Barrows

Text & Music ©2025 Sue Grayson
ssgrayson66@gmail.com

Illustrations ©2025 Laurie Barrows

"Making the World a Happier Place, One Smile at a Time" ™
www.LaurieBarrows.com
corgigrrl@me.com

ISBN: 9798341022713

Printed in the United States of America

Published in the United States of America

MAGGIE MAY
LOVE

HANNAH
MEH

ADDIE
MISCHIEF

SETH
BUDDY

ROSCOE
HUNTER

SKYE
KISSES

NEMI
PARKOUR

LOVE AT FIRST SIGHT

Weeell, the angels in Heaven Nana, and before I knew it, they sent me here to be with you.
I truly believe that buddy. I thank God and the angels for sending you to me.
You're welcome Nana.

Since then our dog family has grown quite a bit. We adopted Skye, Hannah and Addie.

GOOD MORNING

BALL

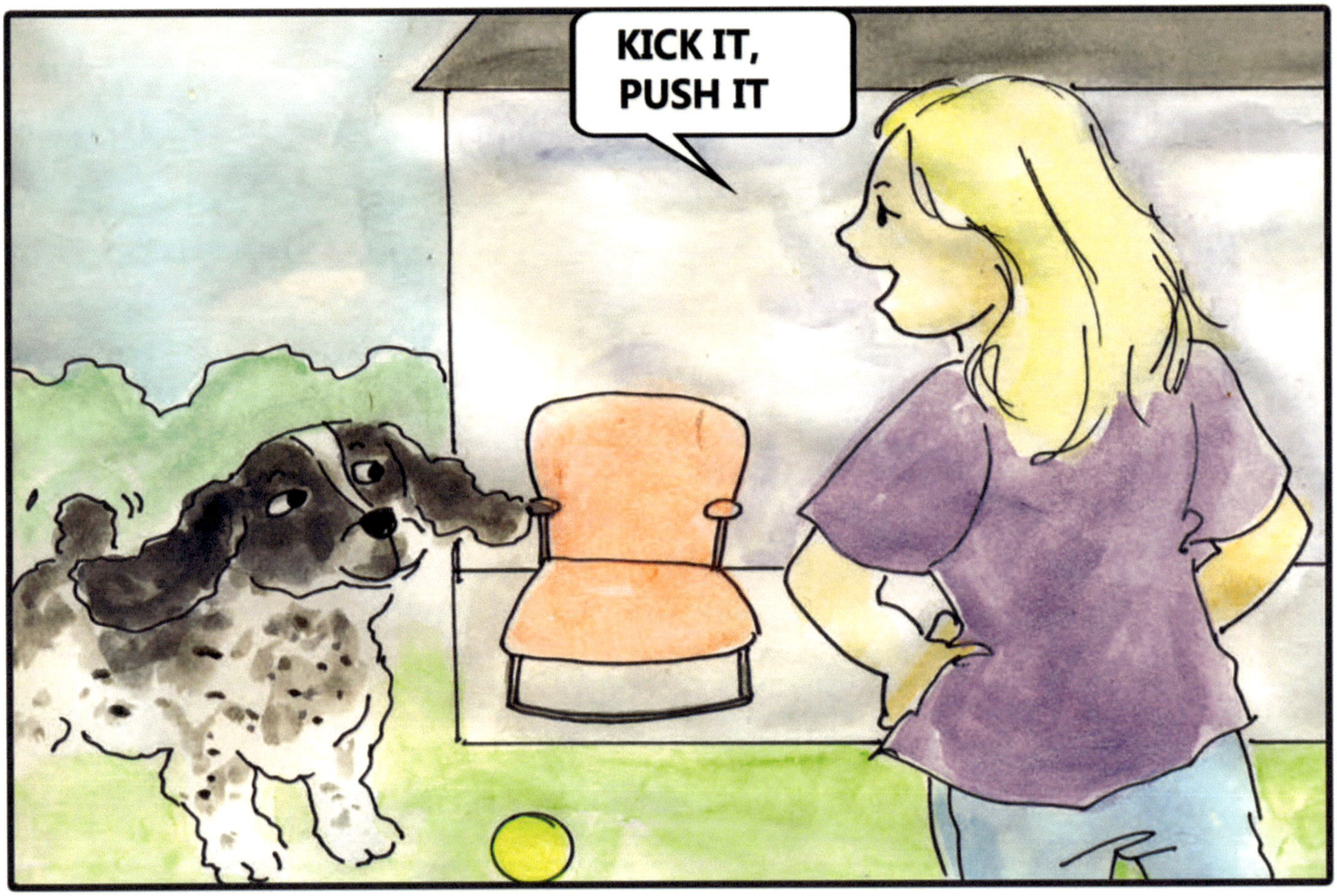
KICK IT,
PUSH IT

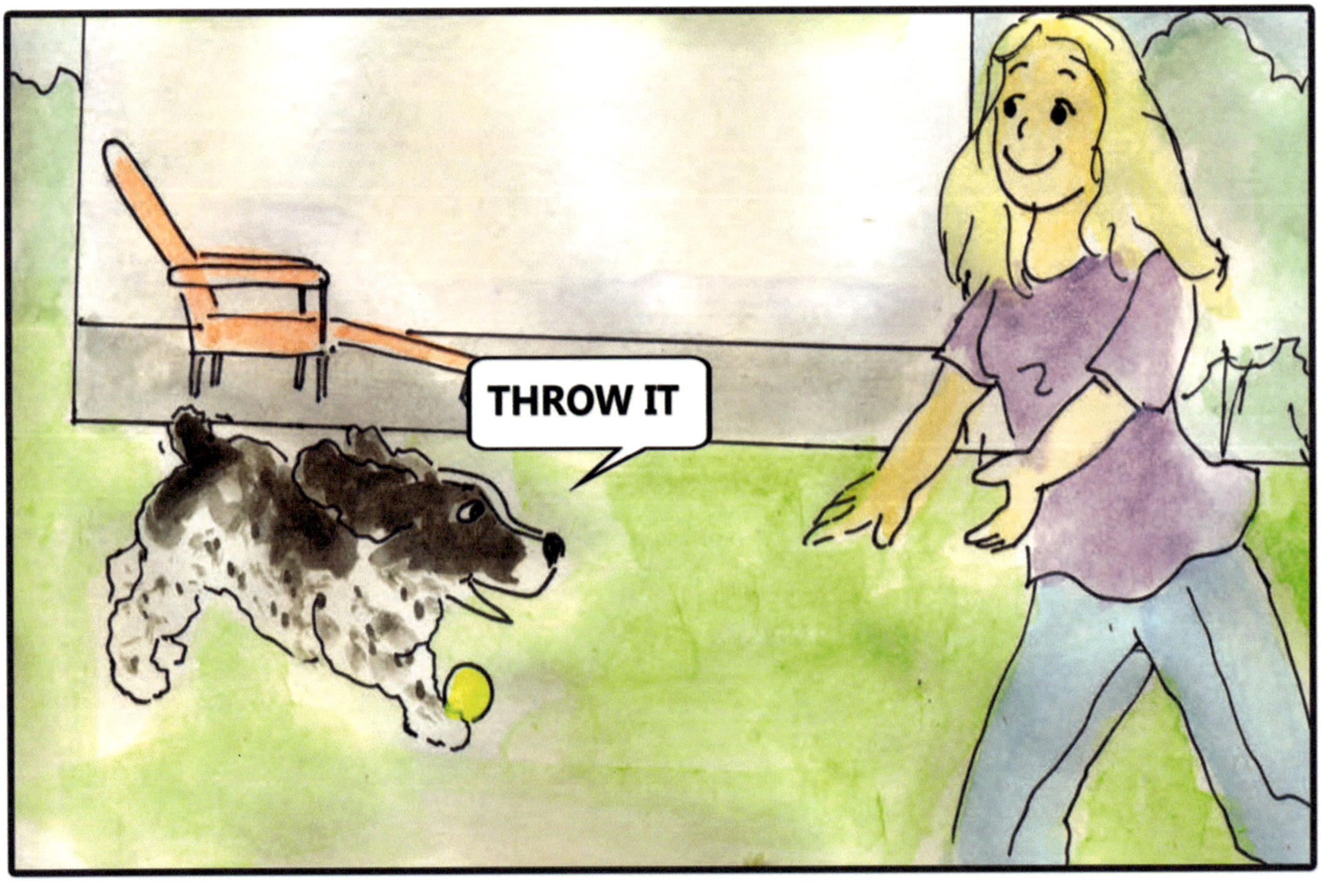
THROW IT

OOPS

PUPPY

OH BOY

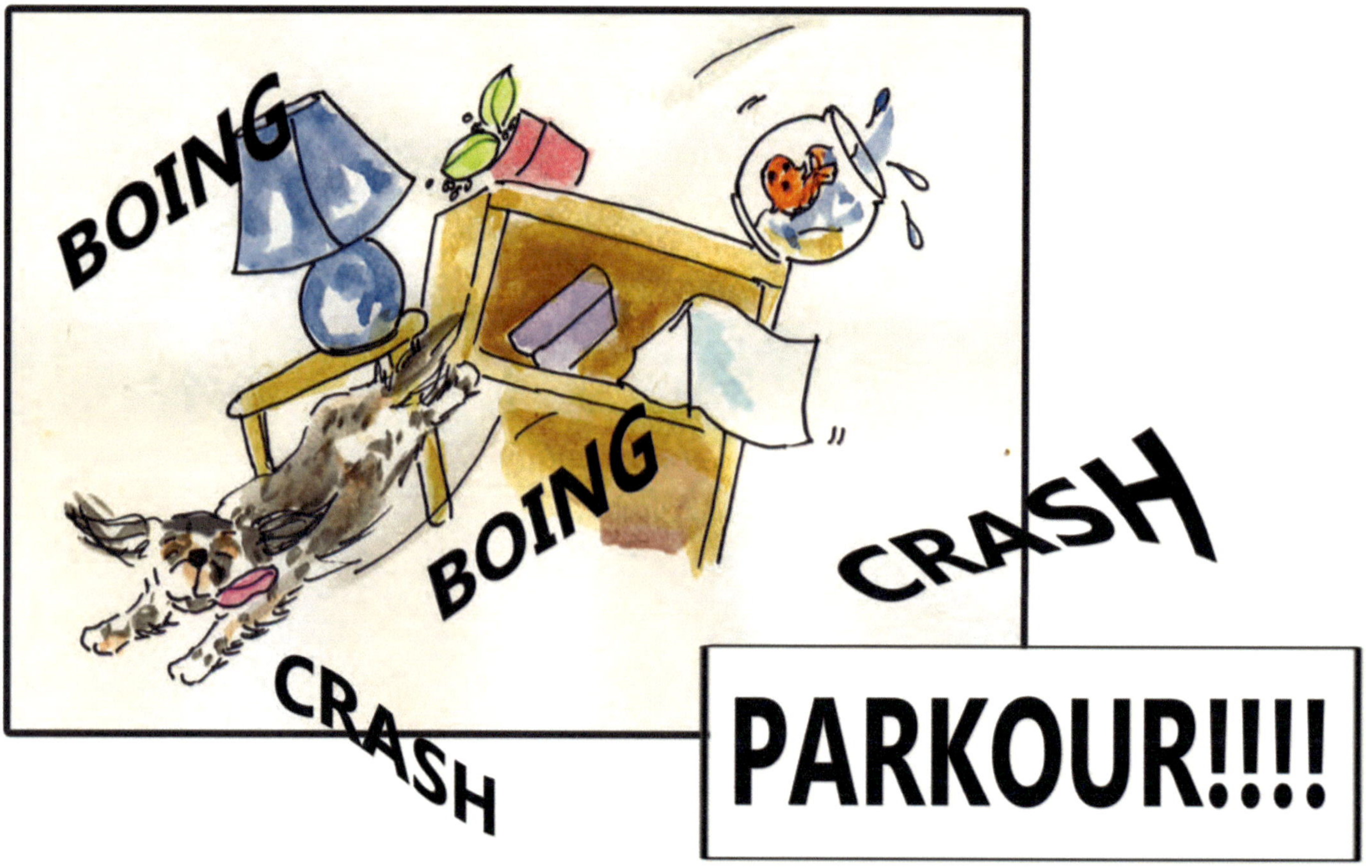
BOING
BOING
CRASH
CRASH
PARKOUR!!!!

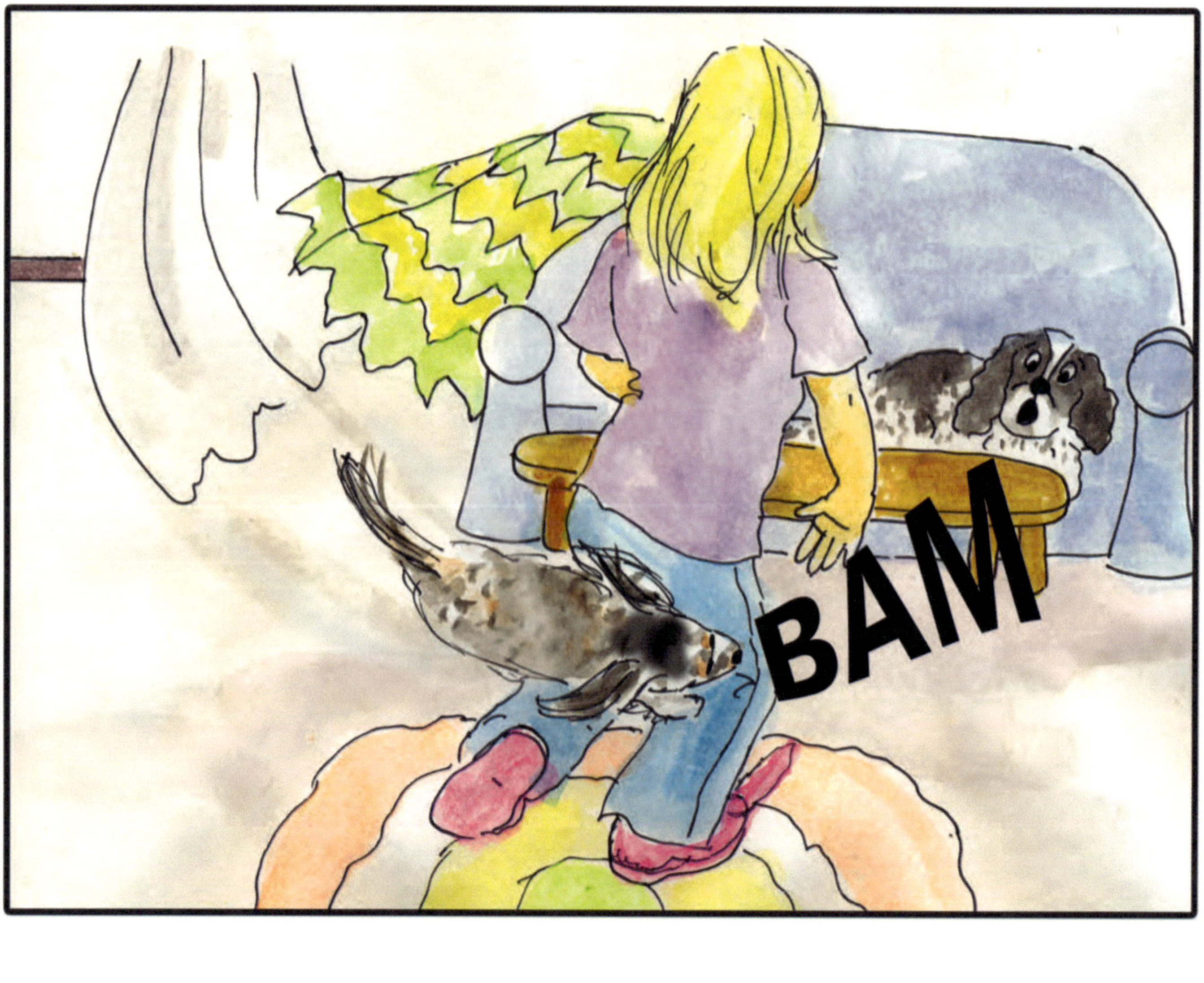
BAM

RIDE

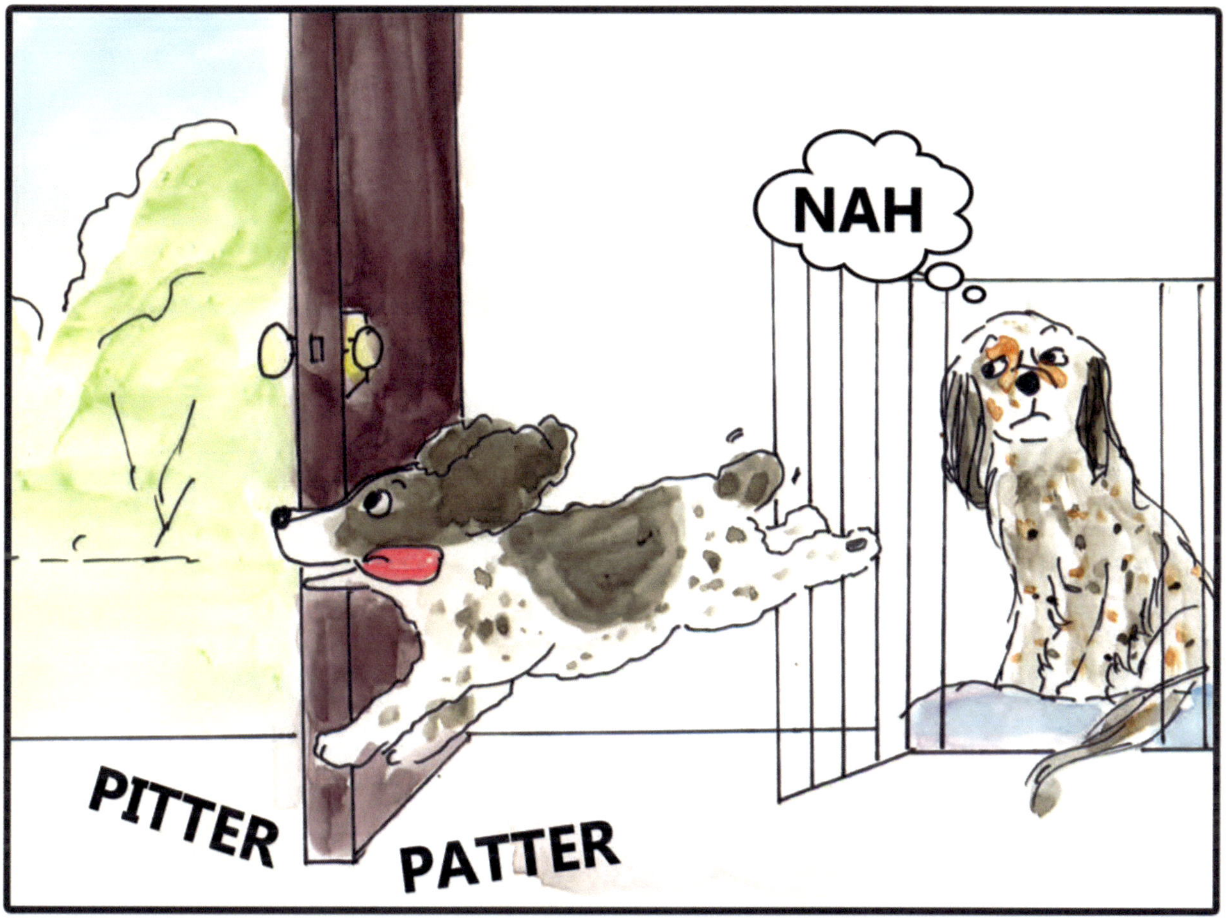
NAH
PITTER
PATTER

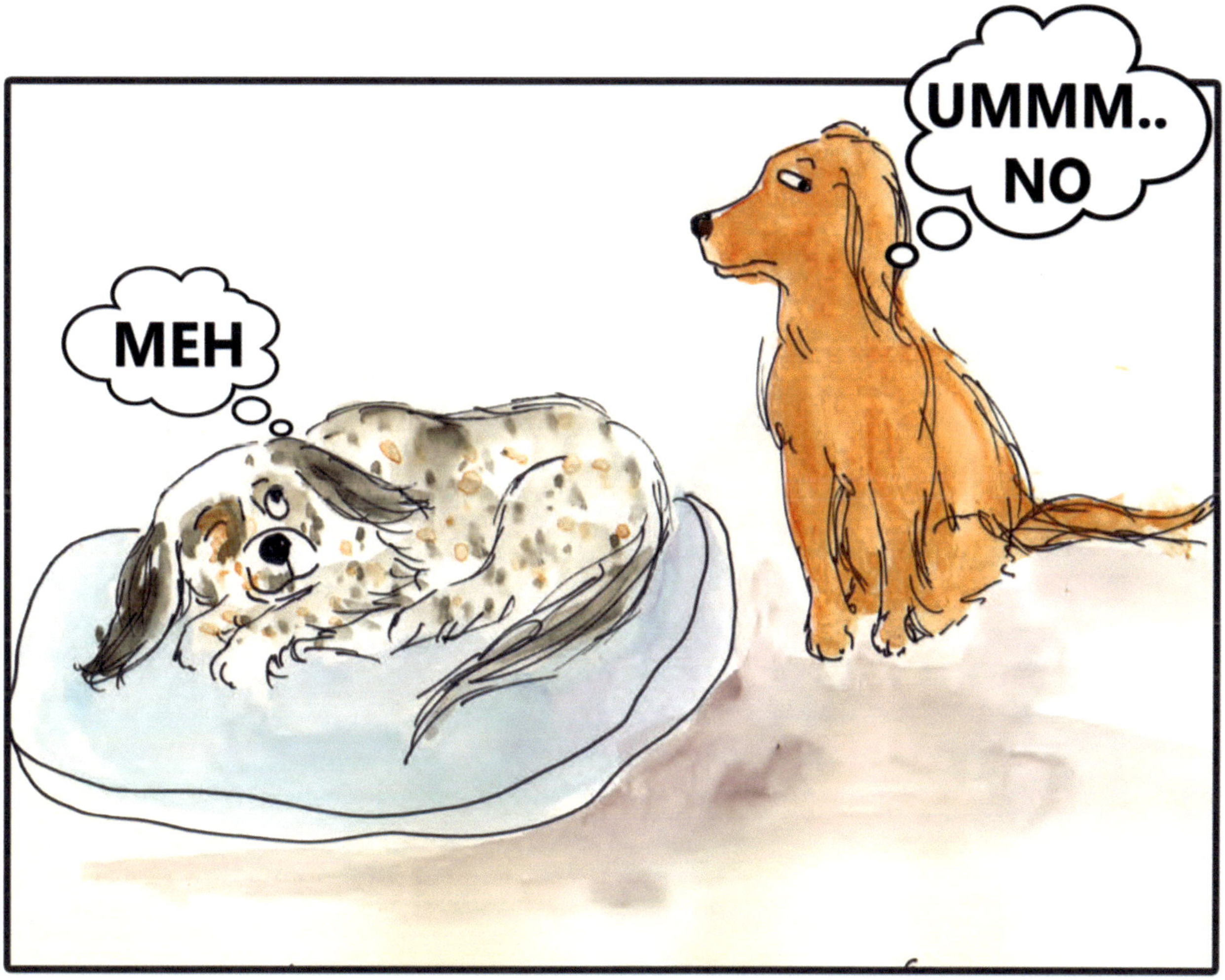
UMMM..
NO
MEH

ROSCOE PUPPY

SNORT

DOOR

HEAVENLY VISIT

TONGUE

FIREPLACE

PAW

AW PAW PAW PAW

PAW PAW PAW

AW PAW PAW

SHUFFLE

SHUFFLE

SHUFFLE

PAW PAW........

FLAT TIRE

YAK

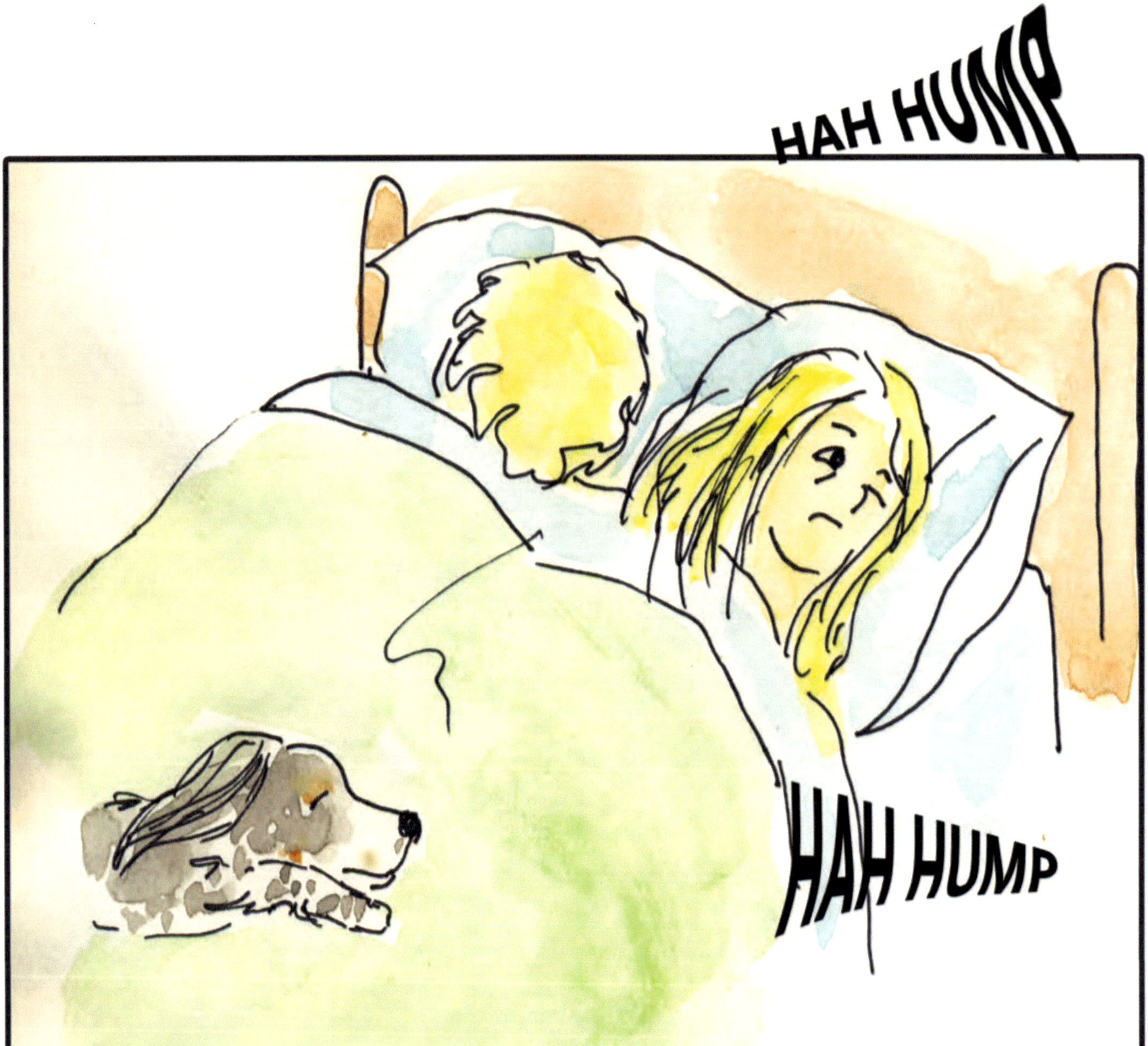
HAH HUMP
HAH HUMP

TAG
TEAM
RELAY

WHAT

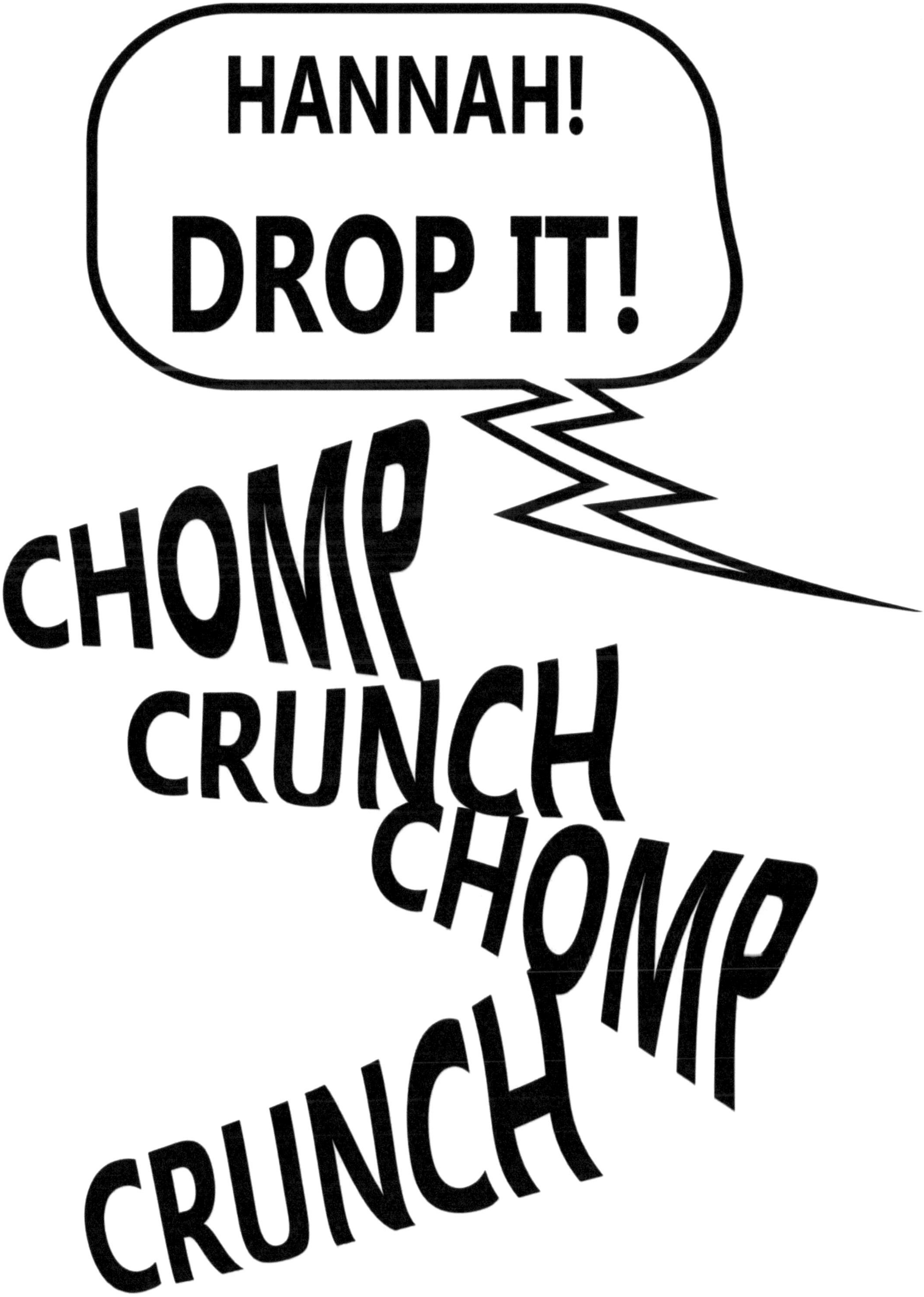
HANNAH!
DROP IT!
CHOMP
CRUNCH
CHOMP
CRUNCH

CIRCUS RIDE

SWOOSH

THE RICKITY ROCKITY ROAD

The Rickity Rockity Road

Lyricist Sue Grayson

Composer Sue Grayson
Arranged by Sue Grayson

THE RI - CKI - TY RO - CKI - TY ROAD.

THE RI - CKI - TY RO - CKI TY ROAD.

THE RI - CKI - TY RO - CKI - TY RI - CKI - TY RO - CKI-

-TY RI - CKI - TY RO - CKI - TY ROAD.

WHO?

INVISIBLE

SHELTIE

RUHRUH
RUHRUH
RUHRUH
RUHRUH
BABIES? PEE WEE AND AUNT LIZZIE ARE HERE.

MEH

ZOOMIES

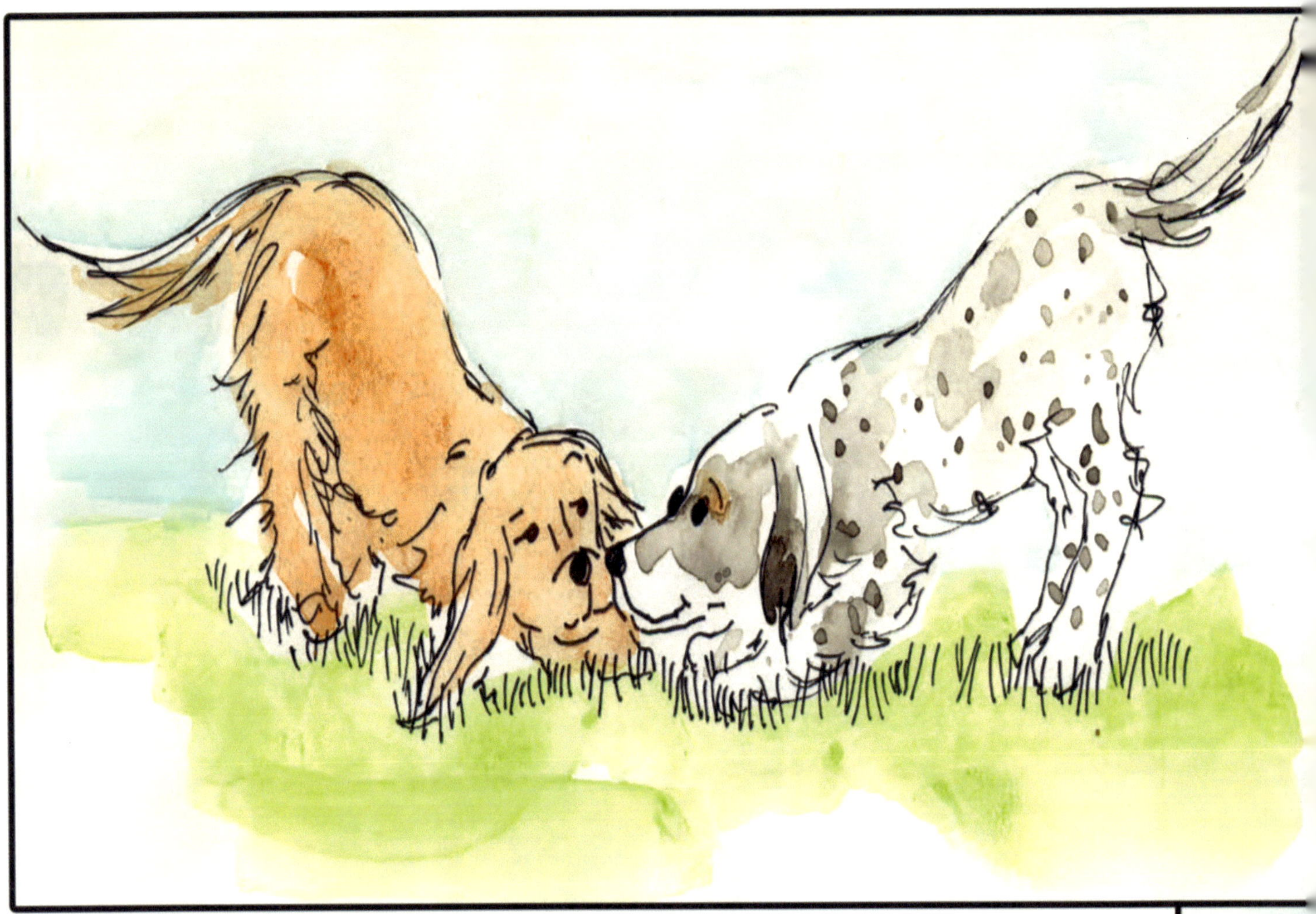

ESSENCE OF DOG

BARK BARK IT'S TIME TO BARK

BARK BARK IT'S TIME TO BARK

Have a lot of fun with this song. I wrote this song to involve interactions and reactions between members of the choir and the soloists, like in a musical. Dog costumes can be used to add to the fun.

Below are suggestions on how to perform Bark.

Verse 1: The whole choir sings.
Verse 2 : Dog solo 1. Choir members turn to listen to dog soloist 1 tell the story. Reactions and interactions would be waving of hands, plugging noses, sympathy.
Verse 3: Dog solo 2. Choir members turn to listen to dog soloist 2 tell the story. Reactions and interactions would be tons of sympathy and gestures of understanding.
Verse 4: Dog solo 3. Choir members turn to listen to dog soloist 3 tell the story. Reactions and interactions would be that of "how fun chasing a squirrel", excitement, and then ouch when the acorn hits soloist head.
Verse 5: Dog solo 4. Choir members turn to listen to the dog soloist 4 tell the story. Reactions and interactions would be that of sympathy and "oh oh", then sympathy and empathy as soloist explains the love from mom.
Verse 6: Same as verse 1.
Chorus: Where indicated, (misc. barking), lots of fun with this. Different types of barking, small dogs, big dogs, howling dogs, etc. The more the better. Lots of interaction between choir members listening to the stories the dogs are telling.
Use a lot of facial animation and gestures. Have a lot of fun.

Bark Bark It's Time To Bark

Lyricist Sue Grayson

Composer Sue Grayson
Arranger Sue Grayson

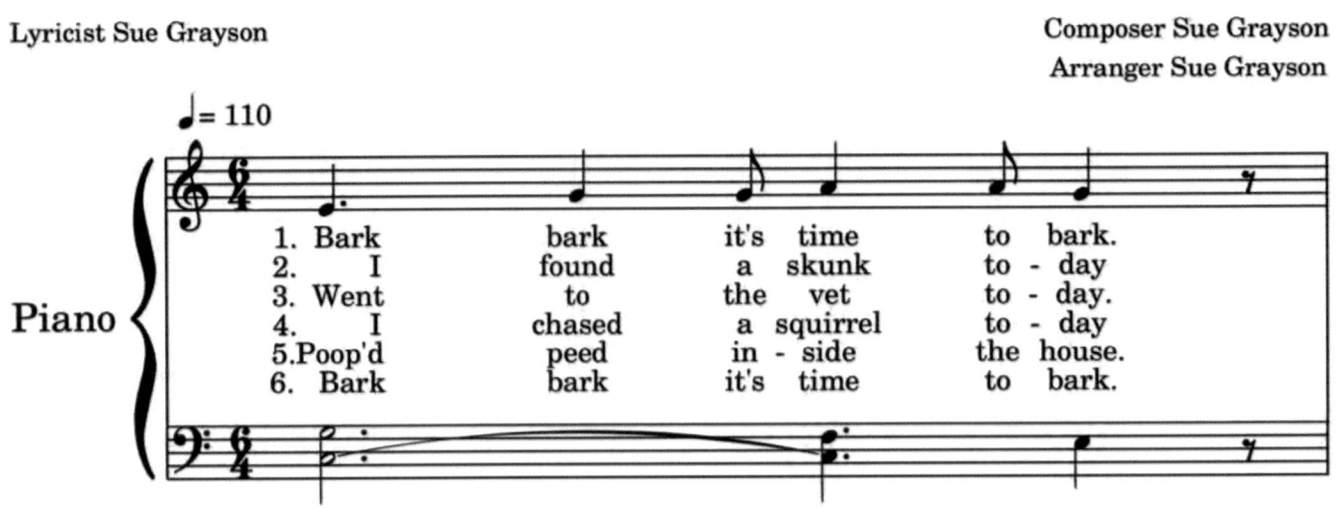

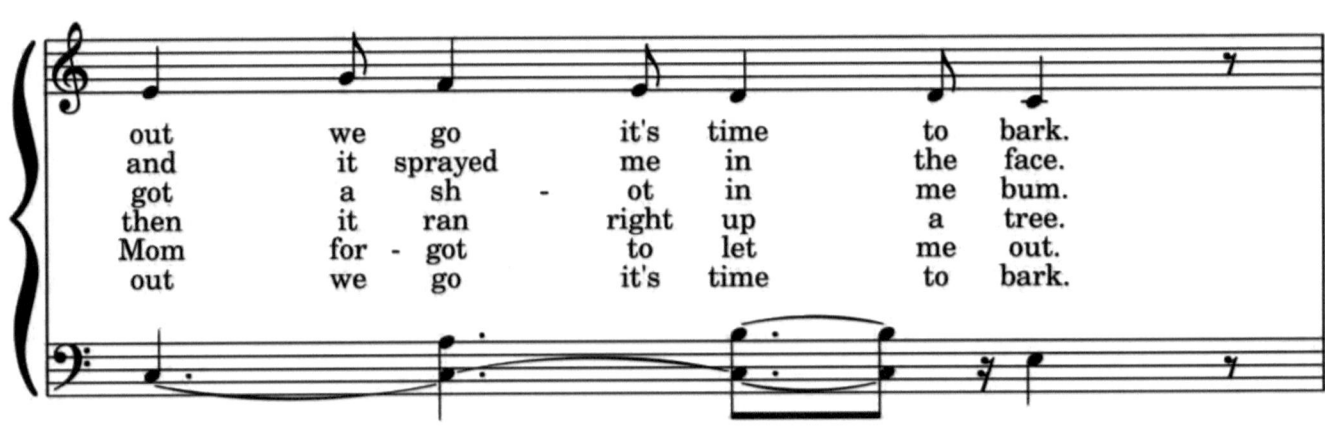

and   tell   the   world   what   we   have   done.
and   rolled   in   dirt   but   I   still stunk.
and   got   a   treat   and   then   went   home.
that knocked   me   out   and   then   it   fled.
she   pat   my   head   and   gave   me   love.
and   tell   the   world   what   we   have   done.

CHORUS   ♩= 133

Ah wooooooo   Ah woooooo   Ah wooo   Ah woooo   Ah woooo

♩= 131   ♩= 120

5x   rit. . . . .   1.

wooooooooooooooooo   we sing a bar-king song

(misc. barking)   (misc. barking)

Seth is on a mission with his Nana to solve a mysterious noise. Follow Seth with his sisters, Maggie May, Addie, Hannah, and Skye, as Nana discovers how amazing they are with their special dog abilities.

ISBN 9798578486210

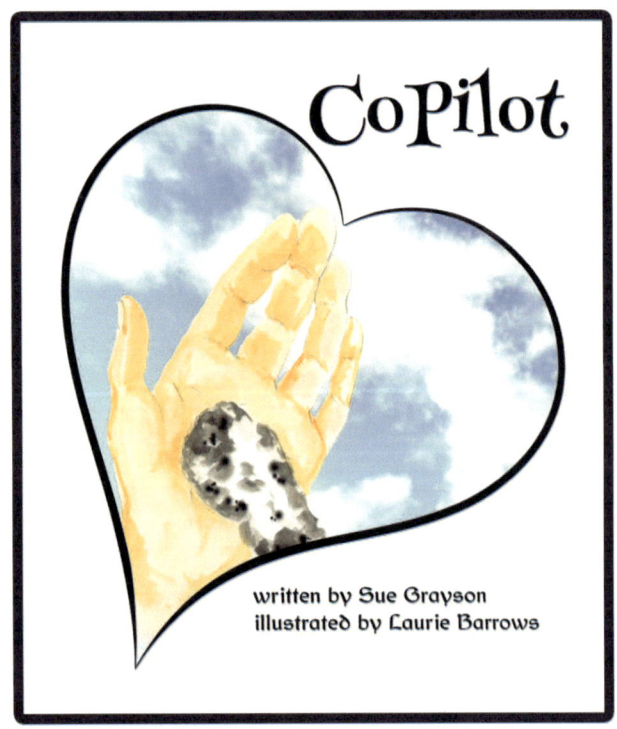

What is it that makes our dogs so special? They possess the ability to capture our hearts and minds by just watching and observing them every day. All of our dogs are Copilots, past, present, and future.

ISBN 9798836594206

ABOUT THE AUTHOR

Author Sue Grayson can't imagine a life without the gift of dogs. Dogs have the ability to inspire us in so many unique and creative ways. She has had dogs all her life and continues to learn about their unconditional love, creativity, humor, and the strength they have in body and soul. She shares the beauty of even the most simple things that dogs do in this delightful book. Come discover these inspirations of dogs.
Irish Setter Skye, Seth the Cocker Spaniel, and orange belton English Setter Maggie May have all crossed Rainbow Bridge, Foster/adopt tri-color English Setters Hannah, Addie, Roscoe and Nemi have joined the family. Sue has been involved in English Setter foster/adopt in the last few years and will continue to do so. Please contact her for information on several English Setter Rescues in the United States. She also has contacts of Cocker Spaniel Rescues in the United States.

ssgrayson66@gmail.com

ABOUT THE ILLUSTRATOR

"Art should be fun!" states illustrator/artist Laurie Barrows.
The artist's work sparkles with playfulness. Bright color
celebrates the joy the artist finds in her subject.

"I carry my philosophy of life into my work. I believe in a positive
attitude and the power of love," says Barrows, "My goal with
children's art is to touch lives with the wonderful luxury of
innocence by creating positive images for the young. Children need
a positive and empowering environment in which to grow and
flourish. Children need freedom to dream. Everyday should be a
celebration of joy and wonder. Developing a sense of self through
play fosters creativity, imagination, and problem solving. We can all
benefit by returning to a simpler time, if only for a moment."
This is her 259th book.

"Success has many definitions. If my work makes you smile, and
brightens your day, I've been successful."

www.LaurieBarrows.com
corgigrrl@me.com

MISSION STATEMENT:
"Making the World A Happier Place, One Smile at a Time."™

Made in the USA
Columbia, SC
10 February 2025

53671470R00137